Impress your friends, family and teachers with super writing projects!

By Gordon Wells

Gordon Wells

Acknowledgements:
Alison Chisholm, author of the best-selling
Craft of Writing Poetry for specially preparing
the section on writing a poem.

ISBN 1-902713-03-6

First published in 2000 by Writers' Bookshop,
Remus House, Coltsfoot Drive, Woodston,
Peterborough PE2 9JX

© Gordon Wells 2000

Welcome - to the world of words

The written word is all around you. Newspapers arrive daily, books fill the shelves, even broadcasters read from the written word. (And for television performers there are written tele-prompts.)

All those words have to be written. By writers.

The written word has a special place in our world. It distinguishes man (men, women and children) from the other animals. Dogs bark, birds sing, wild beasts roar or growl, and monkeys chatter. Insects waggle their antennae - or scratch their legs against their bodies. Even fish make fishy noises. But only man *records* information and ideas in writing. Only man can *preserve* the wisdom of our ancestors.

This book

In this book we will introduce the basic skills needed by the writer. Then we will look at how to use them. First, in writing about what you *know* - reporting on things you have seen or experienced. Or found out.

And then we move on into the world of fiction. The world of story-telling - bound only by your imagination. Find out what it's like to be a super-hero, or a medieval knight. And write about it. Imagine what life is like as a dragon or an undersea monster. Who's to say you're wrong?

As you write more, you will want to show your work to family and friends. Maybe you can make your own magazine - be your own editor. You will also see how to write a poem, how to script a picture-story - and how books get from the writer to the bookshop.

WRITING . . . IS FUN!

This book is easy to read, easy to use. Read it straight through, or dip in wherever you like. Each double page is complete in itself. You can skip forward and back at will. A word of warning though. You cannot forever skip the pages on the basic skills. They've got to be read sometime.

A writer's world

A writer's world is boundless - stringing words together to convey ideas, information, thoughts... and stories. There are so many things waiting to be written. You could write news reports or features for magazines. You could write for radio or for television - plays, news reports, documentaries, etc. You could write fiction - short stories for magazines or full-length novels that go on to become best-sellers. You could write prize-winning poems or verses for greetings cards. You could write books for children or for adults. You could write plays for stage, screen or television.

Whatever your interest, you can write about it. A writer can do anything. And - *writing... is fun!* Enjoy yourself...

'Get black on white.' *Guy de Maupassant*

The writing on the walls

The human race did not arrive on this planet fully equipped with spoken and written languages. These had to evolve, and this took time. People's grunts gradually began to mean specific things. (One grunt for yes, two grunts for no, three grunts for 'Go away, I'm busy'.)

And, just like today, our forefathers couldn't resist drawing on the walls. Early prehistoric graffiti may have been mere scribbles but the drawings soon took recognisable shape.

On the walls of a cave at Lascaux, in France, there are clear, 15,000-year-old drawings of a cow and several horses.

Hieroglyphics

Thousands of years later, the Egyptians were 'writing' on every wall in sight. This 'writing' was hieroglyphic - based on tiny drawings. At first each drawing was self-explanatory - a drawing of a bird meant a bird.

As the system developed though, other drawings came to mean sounds. Thus, a bee plus an eagle could mean b-eagle. Or an eye could mean I. Later still, individual drawings were used to spell out words. On an ancient obelisk, a French linguist, Jean-Francois Champollion, found a series of tiny drawings that he believed to be the king's name, *Ptolmys*. Four of the same drawings appeared again, in another name - suggesting

P T O L M Y S

K L E O P A T R A

WRITING . . . IS FUN!

Kleopatra, the name of Ptolmy's wife. Those two words showed him how the famous Rosetta Stone could be deciphered. He'd cracked the system.

The hieroglyphic names of important Egyptians were framed within oval cartouches. To make life more difficult for today's linguists, these names could be written from left to right, right to left or from the top down.

Why not make your own personal cartouche - using tiny drawings for letters or ideas? Thus, Bill might be a bee and a sick-bed. For Jane, you might want to spell it all out - with perhaps a jam-jar, an apple, a nut and an egg. Your cartouche could be your secret signature.

Meanwhile, there were similar developments in China. Early writing used standardised shapes that we call pictograms. Gradually, these characters became simpler and less obviously pictorial. (Adding a broom to a woman gave the symbol for a wife. Very out-dated now.) Despite simplification, there are still fifty thousand characters in written Chinese.

The alpha-beta

Luckily, some three thousand years ago, the alphabetic system was 'invented' - probably by the Semites. The Phoenicians though, were the first to have just one symbol for each sound. And the Greeks persuaded everyone to write from left to right. The word alphabet comes from the first two Greek letters, alpha and beta. The letter alpha began as a drawing of an ox head which was gradually turned around and re-shaped to form the shape we now use as a capital A.

From clay tablets to paperback books

Having an alphabet was fine, but someone had to use it. The first problem was knowing what to write on. Cave and temple walls were fine but you couldn't take them with you.

In the Middle East people scratched their letters on tablets of clay - then baked them. The Romans chiselled words on lumps of stone.

In Egypt, they wrote on long narrow strips of papyrus - made from pulped reeds from the Nile. They rolled each long strip around a stick and unrolled this scroll to read. (The right reeds were not available everywhere though. Papyrus scrolls had to be carefully stored or they fell to pieces.)

There is a papyrus scroll in the British Museum that is just over 40m long. A lot of words!

Other people began to write on parchment, which they made from animal skins. As parchment improved, people stopped using papyrus.

Scrolls were not easy to read. Smaller wooden tablets coated in wax were sometimes used for book-keeping, two or three being joined by rings. In time, small sheets of parchment were added and eventually replaced the wooden tablets. Before long all the pages were parchment. They'd made a book.

Printed books

At first, all books were written by hand. Few people could read or write.

In Europe, throughout the Middle Ages most writing - and copying - was done by monks. Gradually, more books were produced. Story-tellers' tales were written down and preserved. The Bible became increasingly available. Preachers read it to the people.

WRITING . . . IS FUN!

In China they carved whole book-pages (in reverse) onto wooden blocks, inked them, and pressed them onto paper, again and again. The Chinese had invented paper more than 2,000 years ago - but didn't tell us. And re-usable type. (But each Chinese character is a whole word.)

The Diamond Sutra is the first known printed book. (It is, in fact, a scroll.) It was printed in China in 868 AD.

In Europe, in the 15th Century, Johann Gutenburg invented a press with re-usable type. Each letter was a separate block, so that he could use them to print different words. His first printed book was The Bible - 200 copies.

Once Europe had discovered how to print, many more books were produced. Slowly, more people learned to read - and to write.

Gutenberg's printing press used separate letters, hand-selected and placed in blocks. By the 19th Century, machines could mould a whole line of lead type at a time. When the printing was finished, the blocks of lead type were melted down and re-cast to order.

Today, the majority of people can read. Books are typed into computers. Book pages are then transferred photographically onto thin metal sheets from which multi-page sheets of paper are printed.

Writing style

A sentence is a complete statement. It starts with a capital letter and ends with a full-stop. It is the basic unit of all writing.

If your sentences ramble on and on, they can be difficult for a reader to understand. And boring, too. Short sentences are easier to read, and easier to write. So take the easy way, and write in short, simple sentences.

How short is short? Make your own checks. Count words in a newspaper and in some of your favourite books. Some sentences in the newspaper will be very long, maybe 25 words. Some will be very short, but ten to fifteen words is a likely average. (Count the total number of words: divide that by the number of sentences to get the average.) I am aiming at an average of around ten words in this book. You could well aim at the same length.

While you are consciously thinking about *how* you write, count the words in every sentence. As you get used to it, you will 'write short' without thinking. And they will be easy to read.

Remember though, that an average doesn't mean that every sentence has to be ten words long. Make some sentences short, and some long. Balance them out.

If you use all short sentences, your writing will feel fast-moving and jumpy. All longer sentences and everything slows down. Vary them: it's more interesting.

Short words too

When you are reading, and come across a long word that you don't understand, you probably skip it and hope its meaning will come clear. Too many long, hard words and you may stop reading. Remember that in your own writing. Try to use short words that are easy to understand.

Don't be afraid of using an occasional longer word though. Sometimes it is the only *right* one. You can afford to experiment a bit. Just make sure the word you choose is one that most people will understand. (Who knows what an *oxymoron* is? There has to be an easier way of saying it's a 'self-contradictory figure of speech'. I would always find a way round it rather than write it.)

Paragraphs

Each paragraph should deal with a single topic. If you need to change the subject, start a fresh paragraph. Keep your paragraphs short too - short paragraphs *look* easy to understand.

Your paragraphs can be very short. Like this. (Short paragraphs get noticed.)

Or they can be longer. Vary the lengths but - for now - try not to have any paragraph longer than about four sentences, or sixty words. Count them.

'I notice that you use plain, simple language, short words and brief sentences. That is the way to write English. It is the modern way and the best way. Stick to it.' Mark Twain

Joining the words together

If I isn't using words right, this do be hard to grasp. It is fine to use simple, easy-to-understand words when you write, but you must still use them correctly. Used correctly, simple words in short sentences are easy to understand. Used badly, even simple words may not make sense.

To use words correctly we all have to follow the rules. There are lots of rules. Most of them you'll pick up in your day-to-day life, and by reading as much as possible. A couple of important ones are:

- *Most* sentences need a subject, an object and a verb. ('I am writing this book' - subject, I; object, this book; verb, am [writing].) In some sentences though, the subject or the object may just be implied.

- The verb must *follow* - that is, *agree with* - the subject. I am is correct; I is or I are, are incorrect. (Think: I am, you are, he/she is, we are, you are, they are.)

Short sentences will help to keep your grammar on the right lines. You can spot the errors in a short sentence; it's less easy in a long one. Reading aloud what you have written will also help - mistakes will usually sound wrong.

Spelling matters

Reading aloud won't help with poor spelling. But reading will.

Iff yu rite reel bad lyke thiss peepul wil larf at yu.

The more you read, the better your spelling will get. You will *know* when a word doesn't look right.

CUCUMBER'S 20p

Use short, everyday words as much as possible. They will usually be simpler to spell - and easier to understand. You don't have to use long, unfamiliar words just because you're writing.

Sometimes though, you will *need* to use a longer word - and you're not sure how to spell it. That's what dictionaries are for. Never be ashamed to use a dictionary. I keep mine close by and use it a lot. Check the spelling of simple words too - the ones you *know* how to spell. (I only recently discovered that desparate should be spelt desperate. I'd been spelling it wrongly for years.)

Get the point right

If you write in short sentences, punctuation will seldom be a problem. Just a capital letter at one end and a full-stop at the other. Use commas sparingly, where they will make the sentence easier to understand.

But perhaps the most difficult punctuation mark to use is the apostrophe. The apostrophe either indicates ownership - Jack's bike - or marks the absence of a letter - don't, isn't. Thereafter, the only thing to remember is its, the possessive of it, which needs no apostrophe and it's, the abbreviation of it is, which does. Simple, when you know. Isn't it?

Keep a diary

Every writer should keep a diary. Not for noting future appointments, but for recording the past and present.

As a wannabe writer, your diary should be your best friend. You can - and should - tell it all. It's the place to record what you think about whatever interests you. Record your unspoken feelings, your secret thoughts, your hopes and fears. And, of course, not just the secrets.

An ordinary 'page-a-day' diary is probably not the best thing for a writer's diary. Some days you will not have much to record; other days a lot. A sturdy book of blank pages is ideal. If you are going to record many secrets, you may want to keep it locked away.

Don't, though, write only about the unusual things - secret thoughts, etc. Describe the ordinary, boring bits too. Anyway, for a writer, nothing should be boring.

A source for the future

There is *always* something of interest. If you think not - think again. You are not keeping the diary as a basis for your memoirs. Partly, it is to help you later, when writing stories. It will remind you how you felt when... It will remind you what you had to do when...

Use your diary to record detailed descriptions of people you meet: strangers, friends and family alike. Record what you think of them too. (Don't worry, they'll never see it.) One day, you will want to invent a character for a story. He or she can be based on a mixture of various parts of several of these acquaintances.

To preserve your secrets, you could write your diary entries in code. You would be in good company.

For ten years, 1659-69, senior civil servant Samuel Pepys kept a diary. In it, he recorded his eventful - and often naughty - daily life in London and his most intimate feelings. Wisely, he wrote his diary in his own shorthand. This 'code' was not deciphered until 1825.

But be careful. Too simple a code offers little protection. Parents will seldom be a problem but your younger brother or sister might. They are quite likely to be nosy - and willing to spend time code-breaking.

Too 'unbreakable' a code though, and you may not be able to remember it yourself. Remember, you may be consulting your diary in ten or more years time. (The diary will be of greater use in ten years than it will be next week. It's an investment.)

All in all, it's probably best to write in ordinary English.

Squirrels know a thing or two

But writing isn't only making up stories. Lots of writing is to pass on information - and to do that, you've got to have it first.

One of the pleasures of writing is the collecting of information - about whatever interests you. (The more things that interest you, the more fun the collecting is. And the broader your knowledge, the more interesting a person you become. Just don't be too pushy about it. No-one likes a show-off.)

Once you start noticing, you will find snippets of interesting information all over the place. All you have to do is... collect up the snippets and store them safely. Just like a squirrel.

Many of your snippets of information will be in newspapers and magazines. Wait until everyone else has finished with the paper or magazine, then cut out the relevant item.

Start a scrap-book

Because, at first, you should be spreading your interests widely, the best way to store your cuttings is merely to stick them into a book.

Most stationers sell scrap-books - go for a cheap one, with big pages. If you also collect things people say, or even jokes you hear, you may prefer a simple lined notebook as your store-place. (A spiral-bound one is probably best. Stuck-in cuttings between the hand-written notes may strain the binding of a 'proper' book.)

Later perhaps, as you narrow down your areas of interest, you might prefer to store your cuttings, etc on loose-leaf sheets of A4-sized paper. That way, you can keep similar items together.

WRITING . . . IS FUN!

Sources wherever you look

You will find snippets of information in the strangest places. I have an advertisement giving the history of Chinese 'shoe' money. (Small silver ingots shaped like tiny shoes.) I recently picked up a beer mat containing instructions on making a corn dolly. Breakfast in a holiday hotel was served on a paper place-mat showing the history of bread-making. They were happy for me to take the mat. I also have a photocopied page from a hundred-year-old catalogue of earthenware dragons. (They were sold to finish off the gable-ends of roofs - and I collect information about dragons.)

Newspaper pictures of interesting-looking people and places are also worth saving. With such a picture in front of you, describing a setting, or a story character is easier. (As with information, it will soon become wise to store setting and character cuttings separately.)

Your storehouse of information will quickly become invaluable. You'll find yourself consulting it every time you write something.

'There are no dull subjects. Only dull writers.' H.L. Mencken

Letters that ... pay off

Everyone loves getting letters. When on holiday, be sure to send a card to your best friend. Send Gran one, too. If nothing else, you can say, 'Wish you were here.'

But that's 'ordinary'. Try to make your holiday cards more interesting. Say what the beach, or the camp-site, or the people are like. You don't need to write much - you can't *get* much on half-a-postcard, anyway. Maybe hint at something special. You can tell them more when you get home.

Friends and family are not alone in welcoming letters, though. Many magazines and comics invite 'Letters to the Editor' - and give a prize to some or all of those they use. Why not try for one of these prizes yourself?

Go for a prize

- First, check that your magazine/comic welcomes letters - and gives prizes for them. If it doesn't, look around for one that does. (Sorry boys: there are more girls' magazines welcoming letters than boys'. Perhaps girls read more? Prove 'em wrong, boys.) Try *Scribbler!* magazine, as they welcome letters from writers aged 8-12 years. Each letter published wins a stationery set (great for writing letters!) and the star letter of the issue wins a T-shirt. For further information about *Scribbler!* call 01733 890066.

- Read all the letters in two or three issues of your magazine.

- See how short the letters are. (They will seldom be longer than 100 words - count them - and are usually much much shorter. As an example,

WRITING . . . IS FUN!

this paragraph alone is 45 words long. Your problem will be keeping your letter short - not finding enough to say.)

- Note what the letters are about. There will sometimes be comments on what was in an earlier issue. Others may be about something funny - or even better, something embarrassing - that happened to the writer. (Nearly all editors love letters that make them, and their readers, chuckle.)

- Write your letter in rough first, so that you can count the words, and make sure that it's all 'just right'. Maybe ask someone else to read it through.

- Correct it, then copy it out, in your best hand-writing and post it off. Make sure that the envelope is correctly addressed - 'Letters' sometimes have to go to a special address.

- Now watch for your letter to appear in the magazine. *It won't be next week.* Nor the week after, but don't give up hope too soon. Producing a magazine takes time. Of course, it might not appear at all. Everyone can't win a prize. Maybe it wasn't interesting enough.

- While you're waiting for your first letter to appear, write another. And another. Keep trying - you'll feel really great when you can show your friends your name in print... and the prize. You'll be a real writer.

- Don't stop when your first letter is published. Keep writing to Editors. Try other magazines. Keep collecting prizes. It's a great hobby.

Getting your thoughts in order

By now, all your sentences are clear and easy to understand. But it's equally important that whatever you're writing - letter, school essay, interview report or story - makes sense *as a whole*.

First, ask yourself why you are writing? Do you intend to give information or to persuade? Your answer may change the way you present your points.

If you want someone to come to your birthday party, or increase your pocket-money, start with something persuasive. If you are telling your best friend about your holiday, reporting on the school football match, or telling the examiner about the Peasants' Revolt of 1381, you must grab their attention quickly. Select something interesting to start with. The 'grab factor'.

Make a list

To select a starter, make a list of all the things you are going to include. This will also let you check that you have remembered everything.

Scribble all the points down, as you think of them, in any order. Don't bother with detail: the list is only to remind you, while you're writing.

For a football match report your list might be something like: that first goal, the referee's mistake, how Pete saved the goal at half time, extra time, and the final result. For a party invitation it might be: time and date, entertainment, what to wear, and how to reply.

Think back to your purpose in writing. A persuasive letter is usually straightforward -start by telling your reader something good and then give the necessary back-up information. Maybe you could offer to do more chores for more pocket-money. Then 'hit them' with how much more you want.

WRITING . . . IS FUN!

Re-arrange the list

If your purpose is to inform your readers, you need to grab their attention quickly - and hold it. Here are some ways in which you can arrange your points to achieve that aim:

- Twin Peaks - ideal for putting together a number of barely related 'stories'. Start with something really interesting, don't let it sag too much in the middle and then... end with something else that's also interesting.

- Historic - ideal for explaining how to do something or for straight history 'stories'. Go through all the steps in sequence. (Problem: the start may not be very 'exciting'. To make it 'brighter', perhaps mention the end result.)

- Circular - ideal for history 'stories' or football match reports. Start with some really exciting part of the story, then explain what came before... and end with more about the exciting   part you started with.

Re-arranging your material in one of those ways will make a more interesting read.

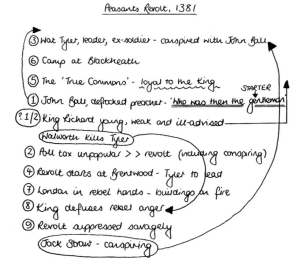

Peasants Revolt, 1381

Polishing your words

We've already looked a little at writing style. And for letters to magazines, you were advised to write in rough - and then check what you'd written.

If you want your writing to be really good, you will always revise. Any experienced writer will confirm that successful writing is not just written - it's *rewritten*. We all need to put a final polish on our writing.

How to polish

How should you polish? What flaws should you look for and correct? Read through what you have written. Try to look at it as though it had been written by someone else.

First, does it actually make sense? Does each section of your writing follow logically from what has gone before? (Imagine this paragraph at the start of this section. It wouldn't be right there. It wouldn't belong. But this is too obvious. You must look for more subtle mis-placings.)

Recalling the earlier advice, about writing style, check the lengths of your sentences and paragraphs. If some of your sentences have straggled on, tighten them up. A mid-sentence 'and' can often be replaced with a full-stop.

Better words

Look for words and phrases where you've said something twice. Once is enough. At the same time, check that you haven't used the same word too often, too close together. Where you have repeated yourself in this fashion,

WRITING . . . IS FUN!

search for an alternative word. (Don't worry: we all do it. But better writers 'polish out' such repetitions.)

If you have used a long and 'unusual' word - a favourite maybe, recently found in the dictionary - ask yourself whether you really need it. Would it all be an 'easier read' if you replaced your favourite with two or three shorter words. (In the first sentence of this paragraph, I changed my initial 'discovered' to 'found'. Just as good, easier to read.)

Look carefully at every use of the word 'very'. (Very often, it's not very necessary. Often, it's not necessary.) Watch particularly for its use to qualify the absolute. Avoid 'very unique'. (That's like being 'slightly dead'.)

Make all these corrections to the first draft of whatever you're writing.

Finally, shut yourself away - in the loo, perhaps - and read aloud what you have written. Properly aloud, not murmured. This helps you identify the phrases that are forced, or pompous. They are not easy to read aloud. Replace them.

When you've done all that, you can say your work is *polished*. It'll certainly be better.

'What is written without effort is in general read without pleasure.' Samuel Johnson

Writers' playtime

We have already mentioned the problems of writing your diary in code. But a secret code would be a real fun idea for you and your friends to use when writing to each other.

Make up new symbols for the alphabet. Be sure to keep a note of what each symbol means though. It would be awful to receive a special letter... and be unable to read it because you'd lost the code alphabet.

An easier code to remember is one where the letters of the alphabet are advanced. Thus, advancing by one, A, B, C, becomes B, C, D. My name, *Gordon*, would be written *Hpsepo*. You can 'translate' it, letter by letter, in your head.

You could make the code more difficult by advancing two letters, or even by retreating. Retreating by two letters, *Bill* would be written *Zgjj*. Have a go.

Puzzles

Another fun thing is to make your own word square puzzle. An eight or ten letter square is about right to start with. Draw up the empty square first.

Choose half-a-dozen words to hide - restrict them to eight letters. Have a theme connecting the hidden words - names of sports or towns, maybe. Letter in the words to be hidden - horizontally, vertically or diagonally in either direction. Let them cross each other.

Fill the empty squares with other letters. Use several part-names to fool people. It's more fun if two of you each make a word square and swap.

WRITING . . . IS FUN!

Consequences

Three or four of you can play Consequences. Each writes a name, real or make-believe, at the top of a sheet of paper. Fold it over, so that the name can't be seen, and pass it to your neighbour.

Now write 'Met... ' and add another real or make-believe name. Fold over and pass on again. Next, write 'At ... ', add a place, fold over and pass on. Write next what you imagine they did - being as silly or sensible as you like. Fold and pass on.

Finally write, 'And the consequence was... ' Again use your imagination. Fold over and pass on.

The pages are now opened and the unfolding stories read out. They should be fun - unless you're not trying.

A	B	C	D	E	F	G
H	I	J	K	L	M	N
O	P	Q	R	S	T	U
V	W	X	Y	Z		

a	s	H	a	o	L		
F	O	O	T	B	A	L	L
O	f	C		O			
U	+	K	G			S	
L	N	E	T	S	L		
T	C	Y	C	L	I	N	G
	A		A				
		B					

Robin Hood

met...Mrs Thatcher

at...the back of the bike-sheds

...they had a fight

and the consequence was... they got married!

What to write about

If you are going to be a writer, you need something to write about. That's obvious.

People will say, 'Write about what you know.' That's fine for grown-ups who have worked their way around the world, invented things or know all about everything. But what are you to write about?

You can still write about what *you* know. About life as a young person in the 21st Century - or how it was in the late 20th. Few grown-ups remember their childhood well. You do. Life is different nowadays.

You are already keeping a diary and collecting interesting bits and pieces. You will soon find things there that you can write about.

Widen your scope

But it's good to spread your interests even wider. Extend 'what you know'.

Decide on a subject that interests you and see what you can find out about it. Maybe you've heard of an interesting person or an event in history. Maybe you've wondered what the universe is made of - or how big it is. Have you thought about where humans come from - in history, myth or... biology? Or maybe you've got a hobby that you want to learn more about.

Whatever your interest, investigate it. It needn't be difficult. Finding out can be fascinating... and fun.

Where to look

Begin in the library. An encyclopaedia is often a good place to start - there are some super ones nowadays. Wherever you look, start with the simplest books. (As a grown-up, I usually

WRITING . . . IS FUN!

start searching for information in the children's library.)

With computers now widely available, you can also consult encyclopaedias on CD-ROM. And, for some things - particularly up-to-the-minute information - the Internet will be your best source.

Whatever sources you consult, make notes of what you find out. Computer information you can down-load and print out. Some information you can photocopy and retain. But there will always be a need to make some notes.

Why?

Remember why you are seeking information, though. It is so that, in time, you can write about what you have found out. You need to be able to consult your notes while you are writing. They have to be close to hand.

But not all of your knowledge will come from books and computers. Some things you must get out and see or do. Don't rely on your memory. Make notes of what things looked like, smelled like, felt like.

Take photographs too. Even if your snaps are amateurish, they will bring back memories of what it was like. They will help you describe it - in words.

'To know all things is not permitted.' Horace (65-8 BC)

You and the 'real world'

If you accepted the earlier advice, you are already keeping a diary of your thoughts and feelings. The purpose of that diary is to be a source of future inspiration, to remind you when you are writing a story of your own.

You might find it a good idea to expand your diary - or to keep a separate section of it - to record what you do, your own activities and achievements. And at the same time note what is going on in the rest of the world - the 'real world'.

Everyone, I am told, remembers where they were and what they were doing when the news broke of President Kennedy's assassination. (I don't know why, but I don't. Like you though, I expect, I certainly remember Princess Diana's death.)

It is always interesting to relate your own life with major things happening in the rest of the world. And it will be much more interesting in ten or more years time, when you read back through your diary.

News items ... and you

So, keep a watch on world and national news items. Make a note of major stories in your diary. At the same time, record what you were doing and where you were - at home, on holiday, at school, etc.

What did you *think* or *feel* about the news story? Were you upset, thrilled, frightened, proud, or what? What is your *view* of what happened, or what was done?

This may not be of great direct or immediate use in your writing. It will, though, help you to develop

WRITING . . . IS FUN!

thoughtful *opinions*. And there is scope for 'opinion-writing'. Think of the 'leader' page in a newspaper. This is full of people's knowledgeable opinions.

Knowledgeable opinions are useful at school too - when called upon to write an essay. If you have a sensible - that is, well thought out - opinion, you will also be a more interesting person to talk to. (Be careful though not to inflict your opinions on those who won't welcome them. No one likes a know-all.)

'News is the first rough draft of history.' Ben Bradley, *American Journalist*

Enlist a friend

As well as your new-found interest in writing, you almost certainly have other fun ways of spending your spare time. A hobby perhaps, or an unusual sport. Many activities and interests benefit from having more people involved. It's usually worth enlisting others.

Of course, you could persuade your best friend to join you in your hobby by just talking it through or demonstrating the activity. In other situations though - with a pen-pal perhaps, or when trying to enlist several people at one time - it is better in writing.

Organise your thoughts

Before you start writing - think. Your object is to persuade. You hope to persuade your reader to join in your interest, activity or club. You must organise your thoughts: be clear, in your own mind, why you enjoy what you are doing. Make a list.

Exactly what do you, in fact, do? And why? What do you get out of it? Will others benefit in the same way or is it only you? What, if any, are the disadvantages of taking up your interest? (Don't overlook this. There is a price to be paid for almost every pleasure. Cost, perhaps, or taking up a lot of time.)

Identify the 'grab factor'

As you know (see page 20), you need to start your persuasion with something really good. As always, you want to grab your reader's interest quickly.

Compare these two notice-board examples:

WRITING . . . IS FUN!

The School Chess Club meets every Monday lunch-time. Come along and learn to play. You will enjoy it - and it will improve your mind.

Can you protect your Queen? Can your Knight capture my Castle? That's chess. It's a great game. We'll show you - Monday lunch-times.

The first example is like many school club announcements. Factually correct but sadly lacking in the 'grab factor'. The second would be more likely to get me there. How about you?

Start with a stirring opening like that. Then you need to explain to your reader a little more about your hobby or interest.

Let's suppose you are a keen athlete rather than a chess-player. It's only fair to tell your reader about the training that has to be put in to get to competition standard. That may out-weigh the attraction of the possible prizes. Again, the necessary fitness may itself be a benefit in other ways. And you meet such nice people. Try to balance any disadvantage with a benefit.

You know that you enjoy what you do. If you hope to enlist others, you have to be persuasive.

Papering the walls

In some countries, daily newspapers are pasted on notice-boards for all to read. You can see wall newspapers in Beijing and other cities of modern China.

A wall newspaper is a good way of 'publishing' news and other factual stories. It avoids the expense of printing lots of copies. It is ideal for any big organisation - club, office... or school.

With your teacher's permission - and help - you could start a wall newspaper at school. For the whole school, or just for your class. All you need is a special notice-board - kept for the newspaper alone - and things to fill it with. You also need someone to be in charge of it. You? More likely, a teacher.

Give it a name

Give your wall newspaper a name. Something like The Green Street Gossip, or Muddleton Murmurings. Persuade someone who is good at drawing to print this title for you, in big letters. Maybe in colour? Pin it up across the top of the newspaper notice-board.

Remember: a newspaper is not a one-off exercise. You will need to keep on providing new material for it. Out-of-date news is no longer news - it's history and doesn't belong in a newspaper. Comment too should be up-to-date.

Ideal things for your school or class wall newspaper include:

WRITING ... IS FUN!

News Items

- School happenings - the arrival of a student teacher perhaps.
- Things to look forward to - important dates, end of term, etc.
- Reports of sports activities - football matches or sports days.

Background material

- School activities - a short report on... the chess club perhaps.
- Interviews - what your teacher, or the school gardener, or... are really like. What makes them 'tick'.
- Opinions - what 'readers' (that is, your fellow students) would like to see happening in school or class. Perhaps, a 'Letters to the Editor' section - but don't expect prizes to be provided.
- Competitions and their results - perhaps the best news report or (very) short story. Or maybe the best poem or holiday photograph. (It may be best *not* to include things done in class. Persuade your teacher to keep classwork separate from the wall newspaper.)

Use bold headlines for news items and background material. Unless you have someone who is really good at lettering, maybe cut out suitable headline words from daily newspapers and re-use them.

The world's first newspaper, the Acta Diurna, *was displayed on the walls of Athens, more than two thousand years ago.*

Goals and home-runs and things ...

Next time you get the chance, go to a big football match. Don't just watch the game. Make notes of what goes on: who scored which goal and when; who got sent off.

Afterwards, think about the match and make a note of your general opinion. Was it a good match? Did the winning team really win, or were they just lucky? Who was the best player - on each side? Why? What was the weather like, and how big was the crowd?

(Don't let your thinking interfere with your enjoyment of the match. But understand that to write about any sport requires concentration.)

Did the press agree?

Depending on how 'big' the match was, there will be reports of it, at least in your local newspaper(s). Read all the reports that you can.

Compare your notes with the newspaper comments. Do you agree on the quality of the match and the players? If not, can you defend your view?

Whether or not you agree with the reporter's comments, notice how the news report has been put together.

A good reporter will have identified the big moment of the match. The decisive moment when it all came good - or went wrong. The report will probably have started with a vivid description of that key moment.

Statistics too

Notice too how the sports reporter has included facts and figures in the report.

WRITING . . . IS FUN!

Readers want more than just vivid descriptions. They want to know that the winning goal was scored in the 34th minute by... with a header, off a cross from... They also want to be reminded that this was the seventeenth goal scored this season by...

To report on sporting events you have to know the background too.

And don't forget the players

A good sports reporter talks to the 'big hitters'. After any sports event you will see reporters clustering around the players - still on the field, in the changing rooms and as they leave.

They are seeking the players' views on the game. They want to hear their excuses. How it feels to have won... or lost. Today's newspaper readers want to know all about the sports stars - their background, their feelings and emotions, their ambitions, even their private lives. Everything.

You are now ready to think about reporting on your next school football or cricket match. You can apply the same reporting principles to sports day - even to a Scrabble tournament. But whatever the sport, you have to work at it.

Make your sports reports interesting. Start with the decisive moment. (The 'grab factor' again.) Include all the relevant facts and figures. Express your opinion - and be prepared to defend it.

Interviewing people

Look in any newspaper. Take note of television or radio news programmes. Many news stories are based on interviews: a reporter has asked the person who knows.

You could interview someone interesting for your wall newspaper. The Head, perhaps? Or maybe the caretaker? Your teacher could arrange these for you.

You will need to prepare for the interview. Decide what you hope to find out - and what the other person might be able (or willing) to tell you. It is wise to prepare a list of questions in advance. Without such questions you could 'come over all nervous' and 'freeze', unable to think what to say.

Sometimes you can find out things about your 'victim' before you interview them. Is there a Teachers' Yearbook or a local Who's Who of your county, including a mention of your Head? Do your parents know any of your Head's out-of-school interests? The church choir, bell-ringing, the local dramatic society maybe? Outside interests give you something different to ask questions about.

Useful questions

Apart from any local questions, here are some that will be useful almost anywhere:

- What made you decide to become a teacher?
- What do you most enjoy as a teacher?
- What was your favourite subject at school?
- Have you had any really good times as a Head? Will you tell me about them?
- I hear you are a keen bell ringer [or ...]. How did you get into that?

WRITING . . . IS FUN!

Make quick but careful notes of the Head's answers. Be sure to offer the Head first sight of your interview report.

You can ask similar questions of the caretaker and of other people, at school and elsewhere. Just adjust them to fit.

Don't forget your grand-parents

Your Grandma and Grandad were born many years ago. When they were young, lives were very different to yours, today. And your grandparents won't always be with you. Find out from them now, what life was like then.

Interview them. They will be happy to tell you all about their early lives. Don't just ask them about their childhood though. Ask them about schools and shops and work - their own and their parents'. (It is not so long ago that milk was brought round the streets in big metal churns and measured out for each purchase.)

They will have much to tell you. Write it all down, in a 'special report'. But perhaps not for the wall newspaper. Maybe you can start a family history book?

Mum and Dad will want to read your report on Gran and Grandad's life. In years to come, you too will want to read again what you found out about them.

'Newspapers always excite curiosity.' Charles Lamb

But you want to write stories ...

So far, we've only been looking at factual writing - *non-fiction*. And learning how to make the best use of your words. But that wasn't really all that you wanted, was it? Your ambition is to write a story. A work of *fiction*.

Writing non-fiction requires you, the writer, to *know* the facts and then to arrange and present them in the best way. Writing non-fiction is about *organising* the truth.

Writing fiction is different. It's about... *storytelling*. You have to exercise your imagination - to invent people, places and events. And all must be believable - within the pretend world of your story.

What makes a story?

All stories are made up of:
- the characters - those who 'act out' your story
- the setting - where (and when) your story takes place
- the plot - what happens in the story - what the characters get up to

And each of these parts is linked with, and affected by, each of the others. They all interact. Because of that, it is difficult to decide which to think about first.

One important thing to remember is that a story mustn't be just real life. In real life, things happen by chance - often, nothing much happens at all. In a story, something *always* has to happen. If not, there is no story. And it is wise to plan the story in advance. Plan it loosely though, because you will want to make changes as you write it.

WRITING . . . IS FUN!

Probably - but there are other views - it is best to invent the characters first. After all, imagine planning a story about fighting alien invaders - and then deciding that the main character was to be... an old lady. Not an impossible story, but getting difficult. (And the more I think about it, why not? At least it would be different.)

Play 'What if ... ?'

Think about the people you meet, the people around you. (People you don't know.) That man over there - could he be an escaped convict? Or a secret agent? Or a millionaire? (He's very smartly dressed and has a large brief-case.) Is he carrying a gun?

The young woman by his side - his daughter, secretary ... or boss? What if they are about to rob the bank across the road? Or maybe she's his wife - but she's very young. Perhaps she's his second wife.

We call this story-making game, playing 'What if ... ?' Play it whenever you can. It exercises your imagination. That's what story-telling is all about.

'Why shouldn't truth be stranger than fiction? Fiction, after all, has to make sense.' Mark Twain

Your main characters

Let's think then, about the characters in your story. Who is the story to be about? There is always some kind of hero (or, of course, a heroine - often both). He or she is *the* main character in the story.

(For the next few pages in this book, let's accept that although many characters can as well be male or female, I'm using male words for them all. But only to save writing 'he or she' all the time.)

There is also a villain - the opposition. Not necessarily an evil person, but someone who tries to prevent the hero from having it all his own way.

The terms, hero and villain, are extremes. The hero doesn't have to be heroic nor the villain really bad. But it's important that there is someone to cause problems for the main character.

There will, of course, be other characters in your story. We'll get to them later.

Be a hero

Put yourself in the position of your hero. Who or what you would like to be, yourself. A comic-book superhero? A major politician? An up-and-coming jockey? A successful athlete, or a budding dancer? A pop star? One of the joys of story-telling is that, in the pretend world, you can be anyone you want to be.

Next, you need to 'find out' all about the new you. To write a convincing story about your hero, you must understand what makes him tick. And the longer your intended story, the more background you will need to know.

WRITING . . . IS FUN!

How do you do?

Describe your hero. Extend this into a brief life-story. Write it all down - in note form.

Where was he born and when? (So how old is he now?) Who were his parents and what did (or do) they do for a living? Where did he go to school and how good was he, at which subjects? What colour are his eyes - and his hair? What sort of a person is he - friendly or a loner, talkative or quiet, lazy or energetic, studious or sporty? Likeable? How did he get to where he is at the start of your story?

Now do a similar exercise on your villain. You need to know him well, too. What is his relationship with the hero? Why don't they get on?

Once you know your leading characters well you will be able to decide on the situations they could find themselves in. You will know too, how they will each react to their problems. Already, you have the beginnings of a plot - a story-line - for your story.

'You can never know enough about your characters.' W. Somerset Maugham

More about characters

Few of us live alone: there are other people in our everyday worlds. In the same way, most stories need more than just a hero and a villain. There have to be others - but not too many. A cast of thousands can be confusing.

Friends and helpers

What sort of story are you starting to weave? Your hero will probably welcome a friend. Someone to help, to talk to, to get his thoughts straight. In the same way, the chief baddie may also need a helper, a fellow-baddie.

Like the main characters, these friends and helpers need to be believable. You must know them well enough to understand how they will act - and react.

You need to know what sort of people they are. You need to know their ages, looks and relationships. Perhaps not in so much detail as for the main characters but enough. Maybe they have a unique gesture, a strange way of speaking, or a physical difference.

Are they extra tall? Do they stutter? Are they forever waving their arms about, knocking things over. These differences help to make them recognisable. Beware of creating bland 'cardboard characters' who never really 'come alive'.

I'm Chloe, who're you?

Think too about the names of your characters. Not just for the friends and helpers, but for the main characters too. Imagine a secret agent called Herbert Witherspoon. Everyone would laugh. James Bond has a

WRITING . . . IS FUN!

better 'ring' to it. But Sir Claude Hartley-Smythe might be the ideal name for a bygone knight in shining armour. Or a nasty villain.

For a present-day story you need to give your characters 'today' names. Not necessarily Chloe and Ryan, but you might be better to avoid names like Edna, Godfrey and Percy. You are usually 'safe' with such timeless names as John and Jane, Anne and Peter. You can have even more fun naming characters in fantasy or science fiction stories.

Think too about how your made-up first and second names go together. (Your parents thought carefully about what to call you - but couldn't change your family name. As a writer, you can.)

Whatever names you give your characters though, you must ensure that they live up to them. Sir Claude H-S must behave like a Sir Claude, just as Chloe has to act the way today's girls do.

Most stories will need other people too. Secondary characters like bus drivers, shopkeepers, or teachers. They are there to support the real story-people. (The sort of person who, in a stage-play, would bring in a cup of tea and say, 'Your tea, sir.') They seldom have to be named and you don't need much detail about them. They can be (good quality) 'cardboard'.

Making life difficult

We know now who our story is to be about. But something has to happen. Something unwanted. There has to be *conflict* - a struggle against something. Without conflict, there is no story worth telling.

What do we mean by conflict? Not necessarily a fight, although that is possible. In story-telling, a conflict can be any sort of problem that gets in the way of the hero. (The villain may have problems - a conflict - too. But a problem for the villain may be helpful to the hero. Problems for the hero are usually more important.)

In story-telling, a conflict can be:

- either physical or mental; (People attacking each other, one way or another - or a mere disagreement.)

- between any two people; (Between the hero and the villain, which is inevitable, because of their 'conflicting' nature. Or maybe a conflict of minds between child-hero and restrictive Mum. Possibly even between the hero and the best friend, who wants to do something different.)

- a struggle against circumstances; (The hero has an accident perhaps and takes time to get better. Or maybe the family cannot afford the cost of him keeping up with his friends. A grown-up may have lost his job - or just realise that he is getting old.)

- a struggle against the environment; (The hero lost in a snow-blizzard or struggling, alone, across the desert could be ideal conflicts for some stories. Being involved in a car crash or a worse disaster would also be an environmental conflict.)

WRITING . . . IS FUN!

- a problem within. (The hero may need to battle with his conscience, or with a feeling of guilt. Or even, a lesser conflict, unable to decide what to do.)

Make the conflict fit the character

Take your main character and think of a fitting conflict. You're starting to get the idea of a story. The conflict has to be resolved - the problem overcome. How? It's up to you.

As and when your hero has got over the first problem... give him another one. And then another. Make the problems more and more difficult. You can even give him several problems to cope with, all at the same time. Maybe there's just one big, overall problem that your hero can only chip away at, merely resolving parts of the problem. Until...

Keep the conflicts coming and the hero surviving them and... you've got the basis of a story. You've got a plot.

'If nothing has changed, it isn't a story.'
Malcolm Cowley, author

Winning through - against all odds

Your poor hero has been floundering around for ages, struggling with his problems. And as he has to survive, he must be overcoming them - winning. It's your job, as storyteller to ensure that the hero's success, his achievement, is believable. (Even magic has to have rules, to be believable.)

Think carefully about how the hero is to resolve each of the problems. Coincidences are only allowed in real life. To be believable, the solution has to make sense - yet not be too obvious. (If the answer is too easy, readers will wonder why the problem.)

Remember that the solving of one problem can itself often cause another problem. Apply that principle to your storytelling. (It may help you think up the next problem to throw at your hero.)

Not only should the solution to a problem be believable and not too obvious, it should not be found too soon, either. (For the same reasons - it mustn't seem too easy.) Keep the reader waiting - in suspense. That's what makes a story gripping.

> *'Make 'em laugh, make 'em cry... make 'em wait!'*
> *Charles Reade, novelist*

Where do we go from here?

Be clear in your own mind where your story is to unfold. It's usually a good idea to have the action take place somewhere you know well - your home town or village perhaps. If you invent a place, draw a sketch map of it - so that you don't have your hero going south down an east-west road that has changed its name overnight.

WRITING . . . IS FUN!

To describe some settings, your collection of pictures of interesting places (see page 17) will come in handy.

The plot has thickened nicely

By starting with a believable hero and other characters, and by introducing - and sensibly resolving - one conflict after another, you have worked out a good plot for your story. A story-line. Write it down: don't rely on your memory. It needn't be more than a few short notes - no one else needs to understand it.

Check it all through again, to make sure it still makes sense.

It does? Fine. You're ready to start writing.

Exactly as you did with your news stories and other articles, you need to start your story with a bang. Something exciting. After that... well you've got it all worked out in your plot, haven't you?

Don't worry if, in the thrill of writing your story, you change some of the ideas in your plot. It isn't fixed. It's there to help you, not restrict you. But if you do change the plot, be sure to check that later events still fit in properly.

A fun way to get a story idea

If you found it hard to work out a plot for your story by playing 'What if... ?' with the characters, and throwing problems at them, here's another way. It's like playing Consequences (see page 25) - but on your own.

You need some plain postcards. (Index or correspondence cards will do equally well.) Cut twelve cards into three - giving you 36 cards, each about 10 cm x 5 cm. It's best if the small cards are all the *same* size.

Divide the cards into six packs of six. Use each mini-pack for a different story-telling element. Write an alternative on each of the six cards.

- 6 first main characters - the 'heroes'. Include characters like Sir Claude Hartley-Smythe (in shining armour, of course), a dragon called Henry, a space-pilot called Captain Starr, a school-girl called Chloe (with super powers)... and anyone else who will fit the type of story you like best.

- 6 second main characters - the 'villains', who oppose the heroes. Maybe a nasty teacher, Brian Wilt (nicknamed 'Lettuce-leaf') a mad professor, Dr. Strange, a 'nutty' robot (called KP, perhaps) with a mind of its own, etc.

  You can, if you like, switch them round. Make the second characters the heroes and the first, the baddies. Your choice.

- 6 problems, causing conflict. Unfinished homework perhaps, or an approaching tidal wave; the need for more pocket money, or an almost empty fuel tank (with nowhere to land except a deserted planet or space-station - or maybe it's not deserted?). Make them up as you wish.

WRITING . . . IS FUN!

- 6 actions - which may resolve the conflict. Running away, or fighting, or just talking, or calling for help or...
- 6 times. Your choice: somewhere in history, or now, or in the future; a whole year or a specific moment (like one minute to midnight on ...).
- 6 places - where it happens. Anywhere from your bedroom to the nearby big town; from outer space to the centre of the Earth; from...

Write the name of the mini-pack on the back of each card - Character 1, Character 2, Problem, Action, Time, and Place.

Big deal!

Shuffle each mini-pack carefully and deal yourself one card from each. Develop your basic story-line or plot from the cards you have dealt yourself. When you've got it right, make a note of it, lest you forget.

Yes, you may cheat - a little. If one of the cards really doesn't fit with the rest, swap it. But don't do this too often. If you already know who and what you want... you don't need the plotting cards.

As you get used to making up story ideas this way, add more cards to each pack. Give yourself more choice. You might want to add one or two more mini-packs. (Perhaps 'The consequence was... ')

I can't 'elp the way I talks

You know what your story is to be about, how it develops… and who wins. All you've got to do now is write it.

Look at one of your favourite stories. The pages contain descriptions of the action - whatever's going on, descriptions of the places where the action is happening, and what the characters are saying. Your story must have all the same three things in it. Without some description, no one knows what is going on or where. And I'm sure you like plenty of action in your stories.

But it's the people talking that really brings the stories to life. You must have dialogue - characters speaking - in your story. And it has to be 'right'.

Listen

Listen to how your friends and family speak. You can often guess who is speaking just by the words they use. The class 'mastermind' probably uses long words - to show off a bit. (And maybe sometimes gets them wrong?) Swaggering 'toughies' will use tough words and sentences - but usually don't sound very bright. Teachers will tell you what to do, friends will ask permission.

Try to have the characters in your story speak in their own individual voices. Ideally, you should be able to recognise them from their words alone. Whatever you do though, the characters must not all sound like you.

You should also strive to write the dialogue in your story so that it sounds natural. In real life, people seldom talk in long speeches - they soon get interrupted if they do. Let your characters interrupt each other too.

WRITING . . . IS FUN!

(To make sure the words sound natural, say them to yourself as you write them - and read them aloud when you are polishing. See page 22.)

Keep listening

Keep on listening to people talking. You will be surprised how often they talk a lot of... er, rubbish. Much conversation is just being polite, or filling in time. Everyone knows what people are going to say before they start. 'Good morning, nice day.' 'Yes, it is, isn't it?' 'Did you sleep well?' 'Yes, thanks. Did you?'

Although you want your story dialogue to sound natural and realistic, you should not include time-wasting chit-chat. You want every bit of dialogue to 'move your story along'. It is not necessary to tell your reader that it is next morning - and then have your characters going through the breakfast table routine, 'Good morning, etc.' One or the other may be useful. Not both.

Good story dialogue has to sound realistic - but be better than real life.

'You can't blame a writer for what the characters say.' Truman Capote

Let's write a poem

It is always a good idea to write about what you know, and most people have some experience of bullying. The physical results can be seen at once. The fear grows inside, but is unseen.

Many poems begin with a word hoard; comments, phrases, rhymes and near rhymes, ideas and thoughts collected in a note book. These are grouped together by meaning or sound, and when you look at the groupings you can see separate bunches of thought. You may use all of these bunches, or drop some of them. While you are making choices about this, a route through your material begins to emerge.

Sometimes you know what form the poem will take before you start to write it. At other times, the first words or phrases you use will shape the poem, These initial ideas did not ask for a strict pattern with a strong beat, but looked for some use of rhyme. Rhyming words do not necessarily have to appear at the ends of lines, but can be scattered internally.

Similar sounds and near rhymes reinforce the poetic 'feel' of the writing. Assonance, (the same vowel sound but different consonants, eg, *green, peep* and *leaves,*) and alliteration, (repetition of consonant sounds, eg, *bruise blooms* and *paints purple,*) strengthen the poem.

Just *get something down!* Staring at a blank piece of paper will get you nowhere. Begin with your 'first thoughts' - play with some words (vowels, adjectives, nouns) you'd like to use and others that rhyme with them. You may not use much of what you write, but your 'first thoughts' will provide a useful starting point and are where every writer begins!

WRITING . . . IS FUN!

FIRST THOUGHTS

A BRUISE IS LIKE A FLOWER
PETALS
BUDS
BLOSSOMS
BLOOMS
LEAVES

PAIN.
VEIN.
FAIL.
RAIN.
PAINT.

KICK
HURT
PAIN —— SHOOTS
WOUND / BURNS
SCOURS

BOOTS

PEEPING THROUGH FINGERS.
THROUGH FEARS?

EMBARRASSMENT -
RETALIATION.
GETTING YOUR OWN BACK
EVERYONE KNOWING.

LEG.
KNEE
ANKLE
THIGH

SEE
HE
FLEE
ME
|
GREEN
SEEN
PEEP
FEEL
LEAVES
SEEP

} EE SOUNDS

BRUISED }
SCHOOL } ∞

BRUISE IS A BADGE -
EVERYONE CAN SEE IT.

BRUISE BLOSSOMS / BLOOMS /
FLOWERS

RED
PURPLE
BROWN — LIKE CROCUS?
ORANGE |
YELLOW   NO - TOO
           SOFT.

SCHOOL BULLY-
NAME HIM. HARD NAME
BRAD. JACKO
STEVE. BILL?
NOT BILL THE BULLY!
BILL THE BRUISER.

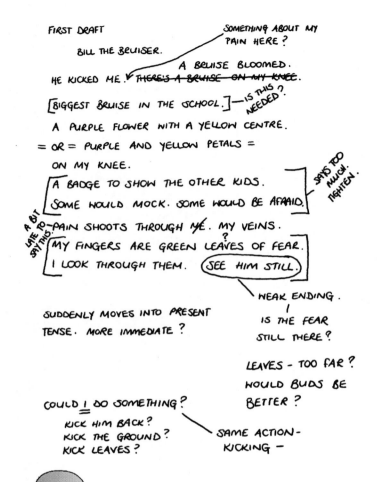

FIRST DRAFT

SOMETHING ABOUT MY PAIN HERE ?

BILL THE BRUISER.

HE KICKED ME. ~~THERE'S A BRUISE ON MY KNEE.~~ A BRUISE BLOOMED.

[BIGGEST BRUISE IN THE SCHOOL.] — IS THIS NEEDED ?

A PURPLE FLOWER WITH A YELLOW CENTRE.

= OR = PURPLE AND YELLOW PETALS =

ON MY KNEE.

[A BADGE TO SHOW THE OTHER KIDS.

SOME WOULD MOCK. SOME WOULD BE AFRAID.] SAYS TOO MUCH. TIGHTEN.

A BIT LATE TO SAY THIS? ~PAIN SHOOTS THROUGH ~~ME~~. MY VEINS.

[MY FINGERS ARE GREEN LEAVES OF FEAR. ?

I LOOK THROUGH THEM. (SEE HIM STILL.)]

WEAK ENDING.
|
IS THE FEAR STILL THERE ?

SUDDENLY MOVES INTO PRESENT TENSE. MORE IMMEDIATE ?

LEAVES - TOO FAR ?
WOULD BUDS BE BETTER ?

COULD I DO SOMETHING ?

KICK HIM BACK ?
KICK THE GROUND ?
KICK LEAVES ?

SAME ACTION - KICKING —

The crafting of the poem continues in the 'first draft', which explores some of the more interesting ideas from our 'first thoughts'. Here we've taken the strongest parts and begun to concentrate more on how they will look when structured into a poem.

WRITING . . . IS FUN!

This subject requires an urgent, immediate approach. The draft's opening seems rather formal. Running on from the title into the first line has more attack and tightens the writing.

The pain appears rather late in the draft. It should be instant, and certainly mentioned before the appearance of the bruise.

Too much has been said about the other children in the school. 'Everyone can see' is all that is needed.

The move from past to present tense happened accidentally in the first draft, but seems effective, so present tense is used throughout the final version.

Changing from 'leaves' to 'buds' of fear implies the start of something that will grow, leaving a slightly uncomfortable feeling in the reader's mind.

A more sinister ending strengthens the poem. 'Boots' rhymes with 'shoots' in the first line, and reflects the image of kicking.

BILL THE BRUISER

kicks me. Pain shoots
through my veins. A bruise blooms,
paints purple and yellow petals
on my knee. Everyone can see.

I kick leaves,
peep through green buds of fear -
see the threat of his boots.

This section of the book was specially prepared by the well-known poet, Alison Chisholm, author of the best-selling *Craft of Writing Poetry* (Allison & Busby, 1992.)

Stories in pictures

Do you read comics? Like *The Beano* and *The Dandy?* Or maybe you prefer 2000AD or *The X-Men?* All these have stories told in pictures - picture-stories. Why not write your own picture-story?

Picture-stories are not new. The Bayeux Tapestry is a 70m long, 11th Century wall-hanging: 72 pictures with Latin descriptions. It is the picture-story of the Norman invasion of Britain in 1066. Today's comics are in good company.

A picture-story is like any other story. A few characters, a problem - and a (fairly) logical sorting-out. Picture-stories in comics are seldom longer than a few pages. That means a limited number of pictures.

For your first picture story, think short. One that you can 'tell' in 6 pictures, on one page.

Picking the piccies

You have your plot. You can't show pictures of everything. Pick the six most important moments in the story. The pictures will show only those - like snap-shots. The reader will guess what happens in between.

Divide a sheet of paper into six picture-frames - three rows of two. In each frame, in order, make a note of the pictures that are to tell your story. The notes can be words, but rough drawings are better. For close-up faces draw an oval with dots and lines for the eyes, nose and mouth. Draw matchstick men for not-so-close action.

Look again at the notes. Will those pictures tell the whole story? Or have you overlooked some important part of the plot? Maybe one of the other pictures is less important? Keep

WRITING . . . IS FUN!

making changes until the whole page is right.

The settings and the action will be shown in the pictures. That leaves the dialogue. Even more than with 'ordinary' stories, this must always move the story forward. And be brief.

As you know, speech in picture-stories is shown in balloons. Two people, at most, can speak in any one picture. In total, not more than 25 words. (There's no room for more.)

The 'picture-script'

On another sheet write the 'picture-script'. Describe what is to be in each picture and write the dialogue. You can also include short notes (captions) to go in the pictures - like 'Next day' or 'Back at home'. (These extras count against the 25 words per picture.)

If you can do it well enough yourself, draw the pictures and put in the speech-balloons. If not, maybe a friend will do the drawing for you - from your picture-script. Either way, the drawings are best kept simple. And you can colour them in when they're finished.

A good picture's worth an awful lot of words.

Example of extract from a picture-script:

Picture 3:	An unfenced country road. Two boys in running clothes. with bags over their shoulders are the hares in a paper-chase. Scattering torn-up bits of paper they cross the road without paying attention. Jack's head is turned, talking to Peter, who is a little behind. Jack has run out in front of a passing car - and is knocked over. Peter cries out.
Caption above:	PETER AND JACK ARE WELL AHEAD OF THE CHASING PACK.
Jack:	WE'VE LOST THEM. LET'S DOUBLE . . .
Peter (shouting)	**JACK! WATCH OUT!**

Your own magazine!

How about producing your own magazine? Earlier in this book we talked about a wall newspaper at school. But you've learnt a lot since then. You could fill a magazine now.

Your first effort should probably be just one copy. If it's good, all your friends will want to read it.

Before you can start work on the magazine it's best to plan it out.

Plan the content

Who will the readers be? Answer: your friends, people like you. So the content needs to be the sort of things you like. These will include many of the subjects of this book - 'news', sports reports, picture-stories, 'stories-in-words' games, etc.

Maybe even 'Letters to the Editor'. (You can have great fun, making them up - from pretend people - for your first magazine.)

Let's suggest a page-plan for your magazine. Let's have two picture-stories, each filling one page (six pictures on a page). Your main story, told in words, might be two pages long. (If you write small, this will be quite a long story. If your hand-writing is large, you may need more pages.) Maybe include another story-in-words - a shorter one.

Most magazines include puzzles and cartoons. Allow yourself a page of puzzles and a page of 'Letters'. And how about a make-believe diary? Not your real diary, of course. You don't want other people to read that!

The puzzles could include a word square (see page 24) - and perhaps a 'spot the difference' pair of pictures.

WRITING . . . IS FUN!

(These are easy to make. Draw a picture. Make a photocopy of it. On the original, remove parts of the drawing - an eyebrow, one finger, the centre of a wheel, etc - using typists' correction fluid. Photocopy the changed original. You now have two pictures - with slight differences for your readers to spot.)

You will also need a cover for the magazine. Think of a good title. And draw, or get someone to draw for you, a big cover picture. Add *splash* headlines of stories inside. Make people *want* to look inside.

Page-filling

Now you can start writing. Prepare each story, report or puzzle on a separate sheet of A4-sized paper. Leave a margin down each side of the pages so that you can 'bind' them together.

Try to write your stories and reports so that they fill the pages. Fill any unavoidable blank spaces with cartoons and jokes.

When it's finished, show your magazine to your friends. If they like it - and they *will* - make several photocopies of the next issue. Sell them to cover the cost.

Good luck - you are now an editor.

'... *the challenge of filling space.' Rebecca West*

From writer to reader

Most non-fiction books (like this one) start with an idea. Before the book is written, the writer looks for an interested publisher to give a go-ahead. If the idea is for a story though, the whole book has to be written before it can be sold.

Most writers work from home, many writing in their spare time. Few get paid until they deliver the finished typescript. And the novelist still doesn't know if his book will be accepted by a publisher.

'I've got to deliver this next week - and I'm stuck!!'

Once delivered and accepted by a publisher, the writer's typescript is checked by readers and editors. It is often sent back to the writer for a few changes - to make it easier to understand.

'I loved it. There are a few bits I didn't understand, though...'

WRITING . . . IS FUN!

The book pages are set up in type. Batches of pages are arranged in large sheets. These are then photographed. The photographs are transferred onto *plates* (metal sheets) from which the book is printed.

'That's the last one for this book!'

At the printers, copies of the large sheets are soon run off the presses. The sheets are folded, the pages bound together and trimmed. And the cover is fitted on. The book is complete . . .

'Let 'em roll, Fred!'

. . . and they are then distributed to bookshops, enabling the reader to get their hands on them!

Over to you ...

The end of the book and I've told you all I can. I hope that I've shown you that Writing... is Fun!

But the only *real* way to learn to write is... to write. Sit down and do it. The more you write, the more you'll enjoy it. All right, you'll make mistakes. They don't matter. You're learning.

Friends may tell you you're wasting your time, you'll never be a good writer. Ignore them - you're *not*, and you *will* be. Find other friends.

All the while you are writing - no matter what you write or how good or bad it is - you are becoming a better writer. You are learning to *love* words. And remember, writing distinguishes us from other animals.

As well as writing as much and as often as you can, you should read a lot too. See how other writers do it. Think how you can copy their way with words. (Don't copy *what* they've written, just the *way* they've written it.) That's how we all learn.

Most important - *keep all that you write*. Store it away safely. In later years you will really enjoy looking back at those early efforts. And you will be able to use your childhood experiences in your adult writing.

You can do it - so get on with it. And enjoy it - Writing is fun!

WRITING . . . IS FUN!

Index

WRITING . . . IS FUN!

You've reached the end of this book and discovered that *Writing . . . Is Fun!*
So how are your drawing skills? What better way to illustrate your own stories and magazine than with your own pictures!

Drawing is not a special gift - everyone can draw - it's just a question of knowing how.
Susie Hodge reveals easy ways to develop your skills and achieve brilliant results. You'll quickly understand how to make your pictures more effective, using practical tips and tricks that professional artists use:

Dividing objects into easier shapes
How to show light and shade
60% looking, 40% drawing
How to make a drawing look 3D
How big are ears?

And lots more - you'll be amazed at how quickly you improve once you start. Have a go at the projects in the book and

ISBN 1-902713-04-4

you'll be able to draw everything from people to perspective, animals to aeroplanes, townscapes to trees. There's even a bit on turning your art into greetings cards so you can really impress your friends, family, teacher - and, perhaps most of all, yourself!